Bryson Dechambeau

BRYSON DECHAMBEAU:
Revolutionizing The Game With Single-Length Irons

Shane B. Gavin

Bryson Dechambeau

Table of Contents All rights reserved. No part of this publication may be reproduced, distributed, or transmitted in any form or by any means, including photocopying, recording, or other electronic or mechanical methods, without the prior written permission of the publisher, except in the case of brief quotations embodied in critical reviews and certain other non commercial uses permitted by copyright law.

Copyright © Shane B. Gavin, 2024.

Bryson Dechambeau

Disclaimer

The following book is for informational purposes only. The information presented is without contract or any type of guarantee assurance. While every caution has been taken to provide accurate and current information, it is solely the reader's responsibility to check all information contained in this article before relying upon it.
Neither the author nor publisher can be held accountable for any errors or omissions. Under no circumstances will any legal responsibility or blame be held against the author or publisher for any reparation, damages, or monetary loss due to the information presented, either directly or indirectly.

Trademarks and pictures are used without permission. Use of the trademark is not authorized by, associated with, or sponsored by the trademark owners. All trademarks and pictures used within this book are used with no intent to infringe on the trademark owners and only used for clarifying purposes.
This book is not sponsored by or affiliated with Bryson Dechambeau, it is just her detailed biography from a very reliable close source , or any Entertainment Industry or political party , or anyone involved with them.

Bryson Dechambeau

Table of contents

Introduction
Section 1: Who's Bryson Dechambeau?
    1.2: Early Life And Foundation
    1.3: Passage Into Proficient Golf

Section 2: Golfing journey
    2.1: Accomplishments at School
    2.2 Achievements on the Professional Tour

Section 3: Exceptional Way to Deal with Golf
    3.1: Single-Length Iron
    3.2: Analytical and scientific approach

Section 4: Actual Wellness And Preparing
    4.1 Transformation And Body Changes
    4.2: Wellness Routine For Golf Execution

Section 5: Media Presence And Public Picture
    5.1: Personality:
    5.2: Interviews
    5.3: Virtual Entertainment Commitment

Section 6: Problems and Controversies
    6.1: Eminent Questionable Minutes
    6.2: Beating Misfortunes

Section 7: Relationship With Fans Friends
    7.1: Fan Interaction

Bryson Dechambeau

  7.2: Individual Golf Player Connections

Section 8: Off-course Projects
  8.1: Business
  8.2: Support
  8.3: Magnanimity
  8.4: Local area association

Section 9: Individual Life
  9.1: Family And Individual Relationship
  9.2: Leisure Activities and Interest

Section 10: Future Aspiration
  10.1: Objectives In Golf
  10.2: Likely Heritage In The Game

Section 11: End
  11.1: Highlights from Bryson DeChambeau's Golfing Career
  11.2: Bryson Dechambeau's Ongoing Effect On Golf

Bryson Dechambeau

Introduction

Bryson DeChambeau, brought into the world on September 16, 1993, is an expert American golf player known for his extraordinary way of dealing with the game. His insightful and logical methodology separates him, as he applies material science and designing standards to his golf swing. DeChambeau's success on the PGA Tour demonstrates his intellect and athleticism in the game of golf by adhering to a data-driven strategy.

DeChambeau went to Southern Methodist College, where he succeeded in university golf, procuring the NCAA individual title in 2015. His unpredictable single-length irons, and indistinguishable shaft lengths for all clubs, mirror his obligation to a steady swing. Bryson DeChambeau got his most memorable PGA Visit triumph in 2017 at the John Deere Exemplary and has since kept on causing disturbances with his strong drives and creative way of dealing with the game. His essential outlook and mission for development have laid him out as an unmistakable figure in the cutting-edge golf scene.

In addition to his accomplishments, Bryson DeChambeau attracted a lot of attention for his physical transformation, particularly the addition of muscle mass that allowed him to drive further. This obligation to wellness, combined with his logical outlook, has reclassified his playing style and acquired

Bryson Dechambeau

him the moniker "The Researcher" in hitting the fairway circles. DeChambeau's journey for advancement stretches out past the course, as he reliably looks for ways of pushing the limits of the game. His effect goes past triumphs, molding conversations about the convergence of science, system, and physicality in proficient golf.

Bryson Dechambeau

Section 1: Who's Bryson DeChambeau?

Bryson DeChambeau is an exceptionally proficient golf player from the US, brought into the world on September 16, 1993. DeChambeau attended Southern Methodist University and graduated with a degree in physics. He was known for his unique approach to the game.

His capricious and scientific mentality stretches out to his golf match-up, where he uses a solitary length iron arrangement, a calculated way to deal with the course of the board, and an accentuation on the information-driven independent direction. DeChambeau's obligation to incorporate science into golf has procured him the moniker "The Researcher."

In 2015, DeChambeau left a mark on the world by turning into the fifth player to win both the NCAA Division I title and the U.S. Novice around the same time. He turned proficient in 2016 and got his most memorable PGA Visit triumph at the John Deere Exemplary in 2017.

Past his victories on the course, Bryson DeChambeau is known for his commitment to actual wellness, as confirmed by his purposeful muscle gain to increment driving distance. His imaginative methodology has ignited discussions about

Bryson Dechambeau

the crossing point of science and game, making him a convincing and powerful figure in the realm of expert golf.

1.2: Early Life And Foundation

Bryson DeChambeau was brought into the world on September 16, 1993, in Modesto, California. He showed early interest in both science and golf, foreshadowing the unique combination of intelligence and athleticism that would become his golfing career.

DeChambeau started playing golf when he was young, and he quickly became a promising young talent. He had a strong work ethic as a child and a thirst for knowledge, both of which would later play a role in his unconventional and analytical approach to the game.

His scholastic interests were similarly noteworthy. DeChambeau majored in physics at Southern Methodist University (SMU). This scholastic foundation not only separated him from a large number of his friends yet in addition established the groundwork for his later utilization of logical standards for his hitting the fairway procedure.

DeChambeau achieved remarkable amateur golf success while attending SMU. This culminated in his historic 2015 season when he became only the fifth player to win both the U.S.

Bryson Dechambeau

Amateur and the NCAA Division I championship simultaneously.

Bryson DeChambeau's initial life mirrors a blend of regular ability, scholarly interest, and a persistent quest for greatness that would eventually shape his unmistakable way of dealing with golf on the expert stage.

Bryson DeChambeau, brought into the world on September 16, 1993, in Modesto, California, has a different foundation that has fundamentally impacted his playing golf profession. Brought up in a family enthusiastic for sports, Bryson tracked down his bringing in golf at an early age.

His advantage in both science and golf became obvious during his early stages. This double energy directed his instructive decisions, driving him to seek a degree in material science at Southern Methodist College (SMU). This scholastic foundation laid the basis for the novel and scientific methodology that separates him in proficient golf.

DeChambeau's playing golf venture picked up speed during his time at SMU, where he made extensive progress in university rivalries. His obligation to the game, combined with a logical outlook, molded his playing style and methodology.

In 2015, Bryson DeChambeau carved his name in golf history by turning into the fifth player to win both the NCAA Division I title and the U.S. Novice around the same time, exhibiting his outstanding ability and flexibility.

Bryson Dechambeau

As he changed to the expert positions, DeChambeau kept on developing, mixing his logical methodology with a devotion to actual wellness. His experience, set apart by an equilibrium between scholarly interest and athletic ability, has situated him as an unmistakable figure in the realm of golf, adding to the continuous exchange of development and technique in the game.

1.3: Passage Into Proficient Golf

Bryson DeChambeau authoritatively entered proficient golf in 2016. Following his fruitful beginner vocation, featured by his noteworthy 2015 season where he won both the NCAA Division I title and the U.S. Beginner, DeChambeau chose to divert proficiency subsequent to moving on from Southern Methodist College.

His expert presentation came at the RBC Legacy in April 2016, where he got it done and tied for fourth spot. This solid beginning promptly flagged his true capacity as an awe-inspiring phenomenon on the PGA Visit.

All through his initial proficient years, Bryson DeChambeau kept on refining his game and gaining insight at the most significant level of rivalry. His cutting-edge triumph on the PGA Visit came in 2017 at the John Deere Exemplary, where he displayed his special way of dealing with the game and got his lady win as an expert golf player. This triumph denoted the

Bryson Dechambeau

start of an effective expert profession that has since remembered different successes and a huge effect on the game.

Bryson Dechambeau

Section 2: Golfing journey

2.1: Accomplishments at School

Bryson DeChambeau's achievements at school are proof of his extraordinary playing golf ability and scholastic capacity. While going to Southern Methodist School (SMU), DeChambeau had a gigantic impact on the domain of college golf.

In 2015, he became the fifth golfer in history to win both the NCAA Division I championship and the U.S. Amateur simultaneously, a record. This shocking twofold triumph highlighted his aptitude on the course as well as showed his ability to perform at the most raised degrees of novice challenges.

His consistency and quiet disposition in university competitions were exhibited by DeChambeau's outcome in the NCAA Division I title. His key and sensible approach to managing the game, informed by his academic establishment in material science, set him beside his sidekicks. His consistent execution of this strategy made it clear that he was one of the most successful beginner golfers during his university years.

Bryson Dechambeau

Bryson DeChambeau's combination of athletic excellence and academic interest during his time at SMU laid the groundwork for his subsequent journey into professional golf, where he continued to disrupt the game with his inventive approach and dedication to pushing the limits of the game.

2.2 Achievements on the Professional Tour

Bryson DeChambeau has achieved a significant amount of accomplishments on the professional golf circuit. He established a major connection with his innovative methodology and strong playing style. DeChambeau has won a lot of PGA Tour events since becoming proficient in 2016.

One of his astounding early achievements came in 2017 when he won the John Deere Excellent, meaning his most essential PGA Visit win. This win displayed his capacity as well as insinuated the erratic techniques he used, including his single-length iron course of action and wise system.

In the subsequent years, DeChambeau continued to establish his presence among the top players in the world. His fundamental usage of data, emphasis on genuine health, and powerful playing style are particularly clear in areas of strength for him, procured thought, and accomplishment. His prosperity at the 2020 U.S. Open at Winged Foot Golf Club

Bryson Dechambeau

was a vital second in his livelihood, showing his ability to prevail on huge stages and under testing conditions.

DeChambeau's commitments to group events, such as representing the United States in the Ryder Cup, in addition to his victories, highlight his influence on skilled golf. His enthusiasm to stretch boundaries and challenge standard guidelines has begun discussions about the combination of science and rawness in the game, making Bryson DeChambeau an unquestionable figure in contemporary golf.

2.3: Remarkable Results in Competition Bryson DeChambeau has performed admirably in competition during the PGA Visit. A part of his enormous victories include:

John Deere Praiseworthy (2017): His most memorable expert PGA Visit triumph, was a feature of his particular way of dealing with the game.

The Northern Trust (2018): DeChambeau was a crucial outcome in the FedExCup end-of-season games, displaying his ability to perform under strain.

The Shriners Clinics for Children are now open: Another victory in 2018 added to his creating overview of triumphs on the PGA Visit.

The Devotion Rivalry (2018): Winning Jack Nicklaus' opposition, The Recognition, further set his status as a top player.

Bryson Dechambeau

2019 Omega Dubai Desert Exemplary: DeChambeau ended up on a European Visit by accident, and he had a good time in Dubai.

2020 U.S. Open: DeChambeau brought back his most vital critical title at the 2020 U.S. Open at Winged Foot Golf Club in New York. In his most memorable performance, he defeated Matt Wolff by four strokes to become the 27th player to win the U.S. Open. He furthermore transformed into the principal player in U.S. Open history to average more than 300 yards off the tee in a 72-opening rivalry.

2020 U.S. Open: DeChambeau won the U.S. Open at Winged Foot Golf Club, one of his most huge triumphs to date, exhibiting his strong and key play.

2021 Arnold Palmer Invitational presented by Mastercard: DeChambeau brought back his second huge title at the 2021 Arnold Palmer Invitational. He squashed Patrick Reed by one stroke to transform into the fundamental player to win the Arnold Palmer Invitational in progressive years since Tiger Woods did as such from 2000-2001.

2023 LIV Golf The Greenbrier: DeChambeau won his most paramount rivalry on the LIV Golf visit at The Greenbrier in August 2023. He shot a course record-tying 58 in the third round and a last-cycle 62 to win the opposition by eight strokes.

Bryson Dechambeau

2023 LIV Golf Chicago: In September 2023, DeChambeau won his second LIV Golf competition at LIV Golf Chicago. He shot a last cycle 63, recalling a 28 for the back nine, to win the opposition by one stroke.

Section 3: Exceptional Way to Deal with Golf

3.1: Single-Length Iron

Bryson DeChambeau's unmistakable way of dealing with golf incorporates his utilization of single-length presses, a takeoff from the conventional variable-length presses normally found in golf sets. This capricious decision mirrors DeChambeau's obligation to a more precise and reliable swing.

In a standard arrangement of irons, each club has a dynamically more limited shaft, bringing about contrasts in swing elements. However, all of DeChambeau's irons are the same length, typically a 7-iron. This consistency permits him to keep a reliable arrangement and swing movement all through his iron play.

DeChambeau's engineering and physics training gave rise to the single-length iron idea. By normalizing the length and falsehood point of his irons, he plans to work on the swing mechanics and make a more repeatable movement. This methodology, while extraordinary, has started conversations inside the golf local area about the expected benefits and difficulties of such an arrangement.

Including his historic victories in amateur and professional golf, DeChambeau's success with single-length irons has brought attention to the potential advantages of incorporating

Bryson Dechambeau

scientific principles into the design of golf equipment and player strategy. His use of single-length irons demonstrates his innovative thinking and willingness to challenge conventional norms in the pursuit of golfing excellence, even though it is not widely accepted.

3.2: Analytical and scientific approach

Bryson DeChambeau is known for his scientific and analytical approach to golf, which distinguishes him as one of the sport's most original and creative players. His game and training regimen are all included in this strategy.

Physical Science Foundation: DeChambeau graduated with a degree in physical science from Southern Methodist College. This instructive foundation advises his comprehension regarding the logical standards of administering the golf swing, ball flight, and different parts of the game.

Single-Length Irons: DeChambeau's use of single-length irons is one of his most distinctive methods. Not at all like customary sets where each iron has an alternate length, his irons are generally a similar length, looking like that of a 7-iron. This decision depends on his conviction that it works on the swing mechanics, giving more consistency.

Analysis of Data: DeChambeau intensely depends on information investigation to adjust his game. This

Bryson Dechambeau

incorporates concentrating on send-off points, turn rates, and different measurements to streamline his hardware and playing procedure. His group utilizes Runner and other cutting-edge innovations to assemble and dissect this information.

Actual Wellness: DeChambeau's analytical approach extends to physical fitness in addition to technical aspects. His purposeful muscle gain and accentuation on strength preparation are determined endeavors to increment driving distance and by and large execution.

Inventive Reasoning: DeChambeau's ability to challenge conventional standards and investigation with flighty procedures features his inventive reasoning. This reaches out to his investigation of ideas like side-saddle putting and interesting preparation techniques to acquire an upper hand.

By joining a profound comprehension of physical science with information-driven independent direction, Bryson DeChambeau has reclassified the potential outcomes inside the domain of expert golf. His methodology sparkles conversations about the harmony between custom and advancement in the game.

3.3: Influence On Playing Golf Strategies

Bryson Dechambeau

Bryson DeChambeau's effect on hitting the fairway methods is significant, affecting players and starting conversations about the convergence of science, physicality, and custom in the game. Here are a few vital parts of his effect:

Single-Length Irons: DeChambeau's utilization of single-length irons difficulties the ordinary idea of changing iron lengths in a set. While not generally taken on, his prosperity has provoked a few players and gear makers to reevaluate the likely advantages of a more uniform arrangement.

Game of Power: DeChambeau's obligation to actual wellness and purposeful muscle gain has reclassified the power game in golf. His capacity to reliably drive the ball great distances has prompted a recharged center around the job of solidarity and physicality in the game.

Information-Driven Approach: DeChambeau's accentuation on information examination has promoted a more logical and methodical way to deal with golf. Advanced metrics are increasingly being used by coaches and players to improve overall performance, fine-tune swings, and optimize equipment.

Advancement and Trial and Error: His willingness to try out new things, like side-saddle putting, shows that he thinks differently than other people do. This soul of development urges others to contemplate their own ways of dealing with the game.

Bryson Dechambeau

Integration of fitness: DeChambeau's blend of actual wellness with hitting the fairway methodology has featured the significance of all-encompassing preparation. More players are integrating strength and molding into their schedules to improve both power and perseverance on the course.

Generally speaking, Bryson DeChambeau's effect stretches out past his singular triumphs, impacting a change in mentality inside the playing golf local area. His methodology urges players to embrace a more logical and logical point of view, cultivating another time of investigation and variation in golf strategies.

Section 4: Actual Wellness And Preparing

4.1 Transformation And Body Changes

Bryson DeChambeau's change and body changes have been a point of convergence of his hitting the fairway venture, essentially influencing the two his actual appearance and playing style.

Actual Change:
In 2020, DeChambeau went through a conscious and prominent body change, acquiring impressive bulk and weight. This change was an essential choice pointed toward expanding his general strength and, therefore, his swing speed. By focusing on actual wellness and muscle gain, DeChambeau tried to acquire an upper hand, especially in driving distance.

Expanded Power and Swing Pace:
The essential objective of DeChambeau's body changes was to upgrade his power game. His commitment to strength preparation and muscle improvement has brought about a huge speed up, permitting him to reliably drive the ball longer distances than large numbers of his friends. This change in approach has reshaped the discussion around the significance of solidarity and physicality in proficient golf.

Bryson Dechambeau

Performance on the Golf Course:

The effect of DeChambeau's body changes is obvious in his on-course execution. His capacity to hit enormous drives has been a characterizing component of his game, and he has credited this freshly discovered capacity to the actual changes he went through. This change in playing style has accumulated consideration as well as added to his prosperity on the PGA Visit, including his significant triumph at the U.S. Open in 2020.

Bryson DeChambeau's change addresses a novel crossing point of science, wellness, and execution in proficient golf. It has ignited conversations about the harmony between customary artfulness and the developing physicality inside the game, cementing his standing as a pioneer in hitting the fairway world.

4.2: Wellness Routine For Golf Execution

Bryson DeChambeau's wellness routine for golf execution is customized to improve his solidarity, perseverance, and in general physicality, with a specific accentuation on streamlining his power game. While explicit subtleties of his routine might develop, the accompanying general standards feature key parts of his wellness approach:

Bryson Dechambeau

Training for Strength: DeChambeau integrates a thorough strength preparation program. Core strength, stability in the lower body, and power in the upper body are all targets of these exercises. Compound developments, for example, deadlifts and squats are possible parts to develop in general fortitude.

Bulk Gain: A prominent part of DeChambeau's wellness system has been purposeful bulk gain. This adds to his capacity to create more power in his golf swing, especially clear in his forceful and strong drives off the tee.

Cardiovascular Molding: Perseverance is critical in golf, particularly during multi-day competitions. DeChambeau's wellness routine probably incorporates cardiovascular molding to guarantee he keeps up with concentration and energy levels all through the sum of a round or competition.

Adaptability and Portability: Golf requests an extensive variety of movement. DeChambeau probably consolidates adaptability and versatility activities to upgrade his swing mechanics and forestall wounds. Yoga and dynamic extending may be important for his daily practice.

Nutrition: Supporting his actual requests, DeChambeau probably follows a cautiously organized sustenance plan. This incorporates an equilibrium of macronutrients (proteins, starches, fats) to fuel his exercises and help in recuperation.

Recuperation Procedures: Given the actual cost of expert golf, recuperation is vital. DeChambeau probably utilizes different

Bryson Dechambeau

recuperation techniques, including kneading, ice showers, and maybe even high-level modalities like pressure treatment to upgrade recuperation among rounds and competitions.

Sports-Explicit Preparation: DeChambeau tailors his exercises to mirror the developments and actual requests of golf. He can directly translate his fitness gains into improved course performance thanks to this sports-specific training.

The growing trend of golfers adopting a fitness regimen that is more athletic and strength-focused is exemplified by DeChambeau's approach. His prosperity fills in as a demonstration of the effect a balanced workout schedule can have on golf execution, testing conventional thoughts of the game.

Bryson Dechambeau

Section 5: Media Presence And Public Picture

5.1: Personality:

Bryson DeChambeau has a compelling combination of intelligence, perseverance, and a dash of quirky flair. The following are important aspects of his character that can be seen:

Insightful Outlook: Known as "The Researcher" in hitting the fairway circles, DeChambeau approaches the game with a profoundly logical psyche. His strategic, numbers-driven approach to golf has been influenced by his background in physics, which emphasizes precision and consistency in his play.

Imaginative Soul: DeChambeau won't hesitate to challenge conventional standards in golf. From his single-length irons to his novel wellness and preparing strategies, he grandstands a creative soul. This ability to trial and push limits has accumulated consideration and started conversations inside the hitting the fairway local area.

Serious Drive: Fundamental DeChambeau's cerebral methodology is a furious cutthroat drive. Whether taking a stab at triumph in competitions or expecting to outdrive contenders with his strong swings, he displays a steady assurance to prevail on the course.

Bryson Dechambeau

Energy for Development: DeChambeau's obligation to consistent improvement is apparent in his way of dealing with the two his golf match-ups and actual wellness. A passion for the sport and a desire to challenge himself is reflected in his unwavering determination to improve every aspect of his performance.

Confidence: DeChambeau's personality is marked by self-assurance. Whether confronting testing shots or pursuing striking choices on the course, he oozes confidence. This certainty reaches out to his confidence in the adequacy of his special strategies and methods.

Frank Nature: DeChambeau isn't bashful about offering his viewpoints, and his straightforward nature has added a component of authenticity to his public persona. Whether examining his game, gear inclinations, or the condition of golf, he furnishes experiences with a direct and unfiltered approach.

Commitment with Fans: Notwithstanding his logical way to deal with the game, DeChambeau draws in with fans on an individual level. His cooperation via web-based entertainment and his endeavors to interface with the crowd add to an interesting and receptive part of his character.

Fundamentally, Bryson DeChambeau's character is an intriguing mix of keenness, development, and intensity. His influence extends beyond the fairways, influencing

Bryson Dechambeau

discussions regarding the role that science plays in golf and the changing nature of the game.

5.2: Interviews

Bryson DeChambeau's meetings offer a brief look into the psyche of a golf player who consolidates logical accuracy with a serious soul. The following are some notable recurring themes in his interviews:

Logical Methodology: DeChambeau frequently talks about how he approaches golf analytically and scientifically. He digs into the specialized parts of his game, making sense of how he applies standards of material science and design to upgrade his swing, hardware, and general execution.

Inventive Strategies: During interviews, DeChambeau frequently expounds on his capricious procedures, for example, the utilization of single-length irons. He shows a willingness to experiment and innovate in order to gain an advantage over the competition by providing insight into the reasons behind these choices.

Actual Change: Conversations about his deliberate body change are normal in interviews. DeChambeau subtleties the purposes for his choice to acquire bulk, underlining the effect on his power game and driving distance.

Bryson Dechambeau

Outlook and System: Interviews with DeChambeau dive into his outlook on the course and his essential way of dealing with various competitions and difficulties. He often talks about how he prepares mentally, how he makes decisions, and how important it is to have confidence in your game.

Serious Soul: His meetings feature major areas of strength for a soul. Whether considering past triumphs or examining forthcoming competitions, DeChambeau communicates a profound craving to win and continually work on his exhibition.

Interaction with Fans: DeChambeau recognizes the job of fans in the game and frequently offers thanks for their help. He examines his communications with fans, both on and off the course, exhibiting a friendly side of his character.

Adjusting Custom and Advancement: DeChambeau discusses the balance between innovation and tradition in golf in interviews. He shares his viewpoint on how the game can develop while regarding its rich history, giving significant experiences in the continuous discussion about the fate of golf.

The interviews conducted by Bryson DeChambeau contribute to a narrative that encompasses more than just his accomplishments as a golfer. They shed light on his personality, distinctive approach to the game, and his role in influencing the discourse surrounding golf in the modern era.

Bryson Dechambeau

5.3: Virtual Entertainment Commitment

Bryson DeChambeau's virtual entertainment commitment mirrors his craving to associate with fans, share experiences in his life, and add to the more extensive discussion about golf. Here are key parts of his web-based entertainment presence:

Experiences in Preparing: DeChambeau every now and again utilizes web-based entertainment stages like Instagram and Twitter to give looks into his preparation schedules. Whether exhibiting his extraordinary exercise center meetings or sharing scraps of his golf swing rehearses, he permits fans to observe the background parts of his arrangement.

Promoting Different Methods: His virtual entertainment posts frequently feature the special parts of his game, including the utilization of single-length irons and his information-driven approach. DeChambeau makes a move to make sense of the science behind his methods, encouraging a feeling of straightforwardness and instruction among his devotees.

Associations with Fans: DeChambeau effectively draws in fans through remarks, answers, and intelligent substance. Whether answering inquiries, recognizing backing, or sharing snapshots of appreciation, he adds to a feeling of local area and association.

Personal News: Past golf, DeChambeau shares individual updates via online entertainment. This incorporates looks into his way of life, ventures, and off-base interests. Beyond the

Bryson Dechambeau

professional golfer image, such posts contribute to a more comprehensive understanding of his personality.

Advancing Organizations: In the same way as other competitors, DeChambeau utilizes his online entertainment stages to advance organizations with support and embrace different items. These posts offer a mix of special substance with individual contacts, making a fair portrayal.

Coverage of Events: During competitions, DeChambeau gives live updates and experiences through his web-based entertainment channels. This continuous commitment offers fans a one-of-a-kind point of view on his outlook during contests and permits them to partake in the fervor of his hitting the fairway venture.

Educational Materials: DeChambeau shares instructive substance connected with golf and his preparation theory. Whether separating parts of the golf swing or making sense of the science behind his hardware decisions, he adds to a more profound comprehension of the specialized side of the game.

Bryson DeChambeau's online entertainment commitment is described by a blend of credibility, cooperation, and instructive substance. By effectively associating with fans and sharing both the highs and the complexities of his golf venture, he upgrades the general fan insight and adds to the developing account of golf in the advanced age.

Bryson Dechambeau

Section 6: Problems and Controversies

6.1: Eminent Questionable Minutes

Bryson DeChambeau, a double cross significant boss, has been one of the most polarizing figures in golf for the past couple of years. His unconventional swing, his frank character, and his strength on the course have all drawn analysis from fans and individual golf players alike.

Here are probably the most disputable minutes in DeChambeau's vocation:

His inordinate length:

DeChambeau is known for raising a ruckus around town farther than nearly any other individual on the PGA Visit. As a result, there have been allegations that he is dishonest or employs illegal equipment. In addition to denying these allegations, DeChambeau has stated that he is not "trying to hit it as far as possible."
His long putter: DeChambeau broadly changed to a long putter in 2017. This drew analysis from certain conservatives who accept that the long putter gives players an unreasonable

Bryson Dechambeau

benefit. DeChambeau has guarded his choice, saying that it assists him with zeroing in on his stroke.

His fight with Creeks Koepka:

DeChambeau and Koepka have been involved in a public quarrel for quite a long time. This fight has prompted a few tense trades on and off the course. The two players have made accusations of disrespect and lack of professionalism against one another.

His gradual play: It has been criticized that DeChambeau takes too long to play his rounds. This has prompted a few defers on the course and disappointment among his kindred golf players. DeChambeau has said that he is attempting to work on his speed of play, however, he has additionally said that he doesn't completely accept that he is playing any more slowly than any other person.

His remarks regarding the Ryder Cup:

DeChambeau has offered a few dubious remarks about the Ryder Cup, the biennial rivalry between the US and Europe. He has said that he couldn't care less about the Ryder Cup and that he doesn't accept that it is a "genuine trial of golf." These remarks have been met with analysis from certain fans and individual golf players.

Notwithstanding the contention, DeChambeau is a skilled golf player who has made extraordinary progress on the PGA Visit. He has numerous victories in addition to his two major

Bryson Dechambeau

championships. He is likewise quite possibly one of the most attractive golf players on the planet.

Whether you love him or disdain him, there is no question that Bryson DeChambeau is perhaps the most fascinating and disputable figure in golf today.

6.2: Beating Misfortunes

While explicit misfortunes looked at by Bryson DeChambeau may not be broadly recorded, conquering difficulty is a widespread part of any expert competitor's excursion. Here are a few general focuses that feature the strength and persistence frequently connected with conquering misfortunes in sports:

Injuries: In the same way as other competitors, DeChambeau might experience wounds that can disturb preparation and contest. Recovering from these setbacks frequently necessitates extensive rehabilitation, modification of training schedules, and mental resilience to return to peak performance.

Execution Battles: Golf is a game of ups and downs, and defeating times of execution battles is critical. This could include acclimation to the method, looking for direction from mentors, and keeping a positive outlook during testing times.

Bryson Dechambeau

Analysis and Examination: High-profile competitors, including DeChambeau, are dependent upon public investigation and analysis. Conquering the strain of general assessment requires mental strength, centered around private objectives, and the capacity to involve analysis as an inspiration for development.

Assumptions and Strain: As a fruitful golf player, assumptions and strain to perform at a reliably undeniable level are unavoidable. Dealing with these assumptions, remaining fixed on the interaction instead of results, and keeping a solid point of view on progress add to conquering the psychological difficulties related to exclusive standards.

Changing with the times: Golf is like any other sport in that it evolves. Adjusting to govern alterations, changes in hardware, and developing rivalry elements requires adaptability and a capacity to remain on the ball.

Individual and Expert Development: Beating misfortunes frequently includes individual and expert development. Competitors like DeChambeau might encounter difficulties as any open doors for personal growth, gaining from misfortunes, and ceaselessly developing to remain serious in their field.

While the particulars of Bryson DeChambeau's misfortunes probably won't be widely illustrated, his excursion in proficient golf probably incorporates snapshots of flexibility, transformation, and conquering difficulties inborn in the cutthroat universe of sports.

Bryson Dechambeau

Section 7: Relationship With Fans Friends

7.1: Fan Interaction

Bryson DeChambeau's fan interaction is characterized by a genuine connection with his supporters as well as a combination of engagement, appreciation, and engagement. DeChambeau's interactions with his followers stand out in the following ways:

Web-based Entertainment Presence: DeChambeau effectively utilizes stages like Instagram and Twitter to associate with fans. He provides followers with a behind-the-scenes look into his world by providing insights into his life, training routines, and golfing experiences.

Answering Fans: Whether through remarks via virtual entertainment or connections during occasions, DeChambeau carves out the opportunity to answer his fans. Recognizing messages of help, responding to questions, and offering thanks are standard elements of his fan associations.

Signature Signings: During tournaments and other golf-related events, DeChambeau frequently signs autographs. This furnishes fans with the chance to meet him by and by, get signatures, and offer brief snapshots of discussion.

Bryson Dechambeau

Commitment at Competitions: During competition play, DeChambeau draws in with fans coating the course. He actively contributes to creating a positive and engaging atmosphere by acknowledging cheers, giving high-fives, and interacting with the gallery.

Fan Occasions: DeChambeau has participated in a number of fan-focused events, such as pro-ams and meet-and-greets. These events permit fans to cooperate with him in a more cozy setting, cultivating a feeling of local area and association.

Recognition of Assistance: DeChambeau frequently expresses his appreciation for fans' support in interviews and public statements. The symbiotic relationship between athletes and their supporters is emphasized by a recurring theme of gratitude.

Making Noteworthy Minutes: Whether it's hitting a staggering shot, recognizing a youthful fan, or taking part in fan-accommodating exercises, DeChambeau effectively adds to making essential minutes that resonate with his crowd.

Bryson DeChambeau's fan connection mirrors a real comprehension of the significance of his fan base. By embracing different channels of correspondence, offering thanks, and effectively taking part in fan-related occasions, he fabricates an association that reaches out past the green, encouraging a devoted and connected following.

Bryson Dechambeau

7.2: Individual Golf Player Connections

Bryson DeChambeau's associations with individual golf players display a blend of kinship, contest, and shared regard inside the profoundly cutthroat universe of expert golf. Here are key parts of his communications with individual golf players:

Rivals and rivalries: Like any tip-top competitor, DeChambeau participates in aggressive contentions on the course. Going up against peers energizes a solid cutthroat soul, and DeChambeau's fights with other top golf players add to the show and energy of the game.

Shared Regard: While the rivalry is furious, there is a hidden common regard among proficient golf players. DeChambeau recognizes the ability and accomplishments of his kindred rivals, and this regard is responded to. Post-competition associations frequently include complimentary motions and articulations of esteem for one another's exhibitions.

Group Occasions: DeChambeau works with other golfers to form a team to compete in team events like the Ryder Cup and the Presidents Cup, where they represent their countries. These occasions give chances to build bonds, cultivate a feeling of solidarity, and display an alternate component of connections in golf.

Rehearsing Together: Before tournaments, golfers frequently practice together during practice rounds. These meetings offer

Bryson Dechambeau

a more loosened-up environment for discussions, sharing experiences, and once in a while even cooperative planning for exploring explicit courses.

Friendships outside of class: Past the fairways, golf players frequently share companionships off the course. Whether it's going to occasions together, associating during margin time, or partaking in beneficent exercises, these communications add to a feeling of local area inside the expert hitting the fairway world.

Steady Climate: DeChambeau, alongside his kindred golf players, works inside an expert climate where competitors figure out the difficulties and tensions of the game. Players frequently encourage one another during both victories and defeats as a result of this shared experience, which creates a supportive atmosphere.

Public Corporations: Question and answer sessions, meetings, and public occasions give a look at the connections between DeChambeau and different golf players. Public communications frequently exhibit a blend of well-disposed talk, fellowship, and shared encounters that add to the more extensive story of expert golf.

While the idea of expert golf is intrinsically serious, the connections between Bryson DeChambeau and his kindred golf players exhibit a harmony between contest and brotherhood. These associations add to the rich embroidery of stories that unfurl on the green and then some.

Bryson Dechambeau

Section 8: Off-course Projects

8.1: Business

Bryson Dechambeau, the charming American golf player known for his strange playing style and strong physical make-up, isn't simply a power on the green. He is likewise a shrewd finance manager with a developing arrangement of adventures beyond the game.

UnderPar Life: A Topgolf Contender

In 2023, DeChambeau reported his contribution to UnderPar Life, another idea that plans to upset the golf media outlet. Motivated by the well-known Topgolf scenes, UnderPar Life vows to offer a vivid golf experience that takes care of both relaxed and serious players. The organization's most memorable area is set to open in Stronghold Worth, Texas, in 2024, with plans to extend to 30 areas the nation over before very long.

A Developing Golf Hardware Organization

DeChambeau has likewise cooperated with Cobra Golf to make his own line of clubs, known as the Bryson DeChambeau Assortment. The clubs highlight inventive plans and state-of-the-art innovation, mirroring DeChambeau's

Bryson Dechambeau

obligation to push the limits of hardware execution. The assortment has been generally welcomed by golf players, and assuming a critical part in Cobra's future success is normal.

Past Golf: A Differentiated Portfolio

DeChambeau's undertakings stretch out past the universe of golf. He has joined forces with a few brands, including Bose, BioSteel, and DraftKings, to advance their items and administrations. He has likewise put resources into different new businesses, including an organization that creates man-made brainpower for golf guidance.

A Dream for What's to come

DeChambeau is plainly centered around building an effective business realm. He has a talent for recognizing patterns and opening doors, and he won't hesitate to face challenges. His differentiated arrangement of organizations mirrors his craving to be something other than a golf player, and it proposes that he can possibly make extraordinary progress in the business world.

With his ability, drive, and enterprising soul, Bryson DeChambeau is ready to turn into a significant power in the realm of business. His endeavors in golf diversion, hardware, and the past can possibly change the business and produce significant income. As DeChambeau keeps on extending his business domain, he makes certain to make an enduring imprint on the business scene.

Bryson Dechambeau

8.2: Support

Bryson DeChambeau, a conspicuous figure in golf, has gotten eminent supporters that stretch out past his accomplishments on the course. In addition to enhancing his personal brand, these endorsements influence the landscape of the golf industry. Here are a few parts of Bryson DeChambeau's support:

Cobra Jaguar Golf: DeChambeau has a huge hardware support to manage the Cobra Panther Golf. This organization incorporates exhibiting Cobra clubs and Jaguar clothing during competitions, adjusting DeChambeau to the brand's inventive and sharp picture. His cooperation with Cobra stretches out to special gear decisions, accentuating the collaboration between his logical way of dealing with the game and Cobra's obligation to state-of-the-art innovation.

Bridgestone Golf: DeChambeau endorses Bridgestone Golf balls and is associated with the company. His inclination for Bridgestone balls lines up with the brand's obligation to deliver elite execution golf balls intended to improve players' general game. This support underlines the significant job of hardware in DeChambeau's vital and logical methodology.

DraftKings: DeChambeau has gone into organizations with organizations outside the golf hardware domain, like DraftKings. This cooperation stretches out past conventional

Bryson Dechambeau

supports, displaying his allure past the green and into the more extensive universe of sports amusement.

Lexus: Bryson DeChambeau has joined forces with the extravagance auto brand Lexus. This underwriting bargain frequently includes cooperative promoting endeavors, where DeChambeau conforms to the complexity and development related to the Lexus brand.

Bloomberg Philanthropies: While not a traditional underwriting, DeChambeau's contribution to beneficent exercises, for example, the Bloomberg Square Mile Hand-off coordinated by Bloomberg Philanthropies, mirrors a more extensive obligation to social effect. Such commitment adds to his general picture and brand as a socially cognizant competitor.

Supporters assume an essential part in molding the public picture of competitors, and for Bryson DeChambeau, these organizations stretch out past simple item supports. They address coordinated efforts with brands that share his qualities, whether established in mechanical development, style, or magnanimity. As his vocation advances, it will be intriguing to perceive what his support portfolio develops and the meaning it has on the two his own image and the brands he decides to address.

Bryson Dechambeau

8.3: Magnanimity

Bryson DeChambeau is an American expert golf player known for his lengthy drives and offbeat swing. He is likewise a humanitarian who upholds different causes, including the Bryson DeChambeau Establishment, which assists with becoming the sport of golf for youngsters.

The Bryson DeChambeau Establishment was established in 2019 with the mission to "support junior golf drives to assist with becoming the game, further develop lives all over the planet through the help of youth improvement programs, and give assets to oppressed youth out of luck." The establishment has granted more than $1.5 million in awards to youth golf programs in the US and abroad.

Notwithstanding his establishment and other generous endeavors, DeChambeau has likewise been associated with a few other magnanimous drives. He has joined forces with the US Golf Affiliation (USGA) to advance the sport of golf to youngsters, and he has given his time and cash to help different causes, including catastrophe alleviation and instruction.

DeChambeau's magnanimity is an impression of his obligation to reward the local area and have a constructive outcome on the world. His endeavors to help junior golf and oppressed youth are assisting with guaranteeing that the sport of golf is accessible to everybody and that people in the future

Bryson Dechambeau

will have the chance to encounter the delights and advantages of golf.

DeChambeau's charitable exercises might be restricted. Be that as it may, numerous expert competitors, including golf players, frequently participate in magnanimous endeavors to reward their networks or back causes they are enthusiastic about. Here are a few general focuses on charity in the games world:

Magnanimous Occasions: Golf players much of the time partake in or coordinate foundation occasions, including golf competitions or favorable to arms, to raise assets for different causes. Sponsors, celebrities, and fellow golfers frequently attend these events, which provide a platform for charitable giving.

Establishments and Drives: A few competitors lay out their establishments or beneficent drives to formalize their magnanimous endeavors. These substances permit competitors to zero in on unambiguous causes or local area needs and give an organized way to deal with magnanimous giving.

Community involvement: Competitors frequently participate in direct local area outreach programs, like visiting schools, emergency clinics, or public venues. The purpose of these interactions is to motivate, inspire, and benefit both individuals and communities.

Collaborations with Non-Profits: Competitors might frame associations with existing altruistic associations, loaning their name, time, or assets to help explicit causes. The impact of charitable initiatives may be enhanced by these partnerships.

Raising support Missions: Golf players, as different competitors, may partake in or start raising money missions to help calamity alleviation, clinical examination, training, or other beneficent undertakings. These missions frequently influence the competitor's public profile to support gifts.

Worldwide Drives: A few competitors expand their charitable endeavors worldwide, adding to worldwide causes or teaming up with associations tending to worldwide difficulties.

8.4: Local area association

Youth Effort: Competitors regularly partake in programs focusing on youth, including golf facilities, sports camps, or mentorship drives. These endeavors expect to move and support the up-and-coming age of competitors.

School Visits: Visiting schools to collaborate with understudies, share persuasive messages, and support cooperation in sports or training is a typical type of local area contribution for competitors.

Emergency clinic and Medical services Drives: Athletes frequently interact with local hospitals and healthcare

Bryson Dechambeau

facilities by visiting patients, participating in fundraising activities, or making contributions to health-related charitable organizations.

Noble cause Occasions: Athletes can raise money and awareness for a variety of causes by hosting or participating in charity events, such as golf tournaments, fundraisers, or other activities.

Help for Local Businesses: Competitors might uphold neighborhood organizations and local area advancement drives, perceiving the significance of monetary development and supportability in the places where they grew up.

Natural Stewardship: A few competitors partake in or start natural drives, advancing supportability and protection endeavors inside their networks.

Collaborations with Non-Profits: Laying out organizations with laid out not-for-profit associations permits competitors to use their impact for social effect, resolving issues like instruction, destitution, or well-being.

Magnanimous Establishments: Competitors frequently make their altruistic establishments incorporate and coordinate their local area association endeavors. These establishments might uphold different causes and drives lined up with the competitor's qualities.

Section 9: Individual Life

9.1: Family And Individual Relationship

Golf player Bryson DeChambeau is a confidential individual and has not shared a lot about his family and individual existence with people in general. However, we do know that his parents, Alan and Julie DeChambeau, are close to him. His mother is a successful businesswoman, and his father played golf at the University of Wisconsin-Madison. DeChambeau likewise has a sister named Brittany.

As far as his own life, DeChambeau has been connected to a couple of ladies throughout the long term, including wellness model Nadia Paglieri and sports correspondent Allie LaForce. In any case, he has never freely affirmed any of these connections. DeChambeau is said to be single as of 2023.

DeChambeau is known for his extraordinary preparation routine and his scientific way of dealing with the game. He honestly loves innovation and has been known to utilize information investigation to assist him with his game. Be that as it may, his unconventional techniques have likewise made him a polarizing figure in the golf world. Some fans love his readiness to trial and push the limits of the game, while others view his methodology as excessively mechanical and unoriginal.

Bryson Dechambeau

Notwithstanding the analysis, DeChambeau has been inconceivably effective on the PGA Visit. He has won seven competitions, including two significant titles (the U.S. Open in 2020 and the PGA Title in 2021). He is likewise the reigning FedExCup champion.

DeChambeau is a fascinating and complicated person who will undoubtedly continue to draw attention in the years to come. Whether you love him or disdain him, there is no rejecting that he is perhaps the most extraordinary and gifted golf player on the planet.

9.2: Leisure Activities and Interest

Past his extraordinary ability on the green, Bryson DeChambeau is a complex person with a different scope of interests and side interests. His commitment to wellness and sustenance, enthusiasm for computer games, and innovative undertakings exhibit his multi-layered character.

Wellness and Sustenance:

DeChambeau's muscular physique and impressive power on the course demonstrate his dedication to physical conditioning. He consistently participates in strength preparation, aerobic exercise, and adaptability activities to streamline his presentation. His eating regimen centers around lean proteins, complex sugars, and solid fats, guaranteeing he

Bryson Dechambeau

has the energy and supplements to help his preparation and cutthroat undertakings.

Computer games:

DeChambeau is an enthusiastic gamer, especially partaking in the well-known fight royale game Fortnite. He every so often streams his gaming meetings on Jerk, drawing in with fans and displaying his abilities while likewise unwinding and having a good time. His advantage in computer games not only gives a psychological break from the requests of expert golf yet in addition mirrors his adoration for innovation and cutthroat difficulties.

Expression of Creativity:

Past golf and gaming, DeChambeau additionally fiddles with innovative pursuits. He has communicated an interest in photography and filmmaking, exhibiting his imaginative eye and wanting to investigate new mediums. He has additionally fiddled with music creation, exploring different avenues regarding different instruments and making his own organizations. These imaginative undertakings exhibit his energy for self-articulation and his ability to step outside his usual range of familiarity.

Conclusion:

Bryson DeChambeau is a well-rounded individual with a thirst for knowledge and a variety of talents because his hobbies and interests go far beyond golf. His physical prowess

Bryson Dechambeau

is fueled by his dedication to fitness and nutrition, his love of video games is a source of relaxation and challenge, and his creative endeavors demonstrate his artistic side. His personality gains depth and dimension as a result of these passions, making him a more intriguing and complex figure.

Bryson Dechambeau

Section 10: Future Aspiration

10.1: Objectives In Golf

Bryson DeChambeau's objectives in golf are to come out on top for significant titles, top the world rankings, and become the most imaginative golf player ever. He is an exceptionally aggressive and decided player who won't hesitate to rock the boat.

The way DeChambeau approaches golf is based on data and science. He accepts that by understanding the material science of the golf swing and the biomechanics of the human body, he can work on his presentation. He has been working with a group of researchers and designers to foster a club that is customized to his swing pace and send-off point. He has additionally been zeroing in on expanding his bulk and strength, which he accepts will give him more power and control off the tee.

DeChambeau's objective of bringing home significant titles is aggressive, however, it isn't far off. He has proactively brought home three PGA Visit championships, and he can possibly rival the best players on the planet. He has major areas of strength for a game and he won't hesitate to take on troublesome difficulties.

DeChambeau's objective of fixing the world rankings is likewise aggressive, however, it is feasible. He has the ability and the drive to arrive at the highest point of the game. Additionally, he is in a good position to profit from the rising popularity of golf in the United States.

DeChambeau's objective of turning into the most creative golf player ever is a touch more emotional, however, he is surely doing great. He is always pushing the boundaries of what is possible in golf, and he does not hesitate to try out new tools and methods. He is a trailblazer in the game, and he is preparing people for the future of golf players.

DeChambeau's golf goals are ambitious but also attainable. He has the ability, the drive, and the emotionally supportive network to accomplish them. He is a once-in-a-age ability, and he is just barely starting to start to expose his true capacity.

10.2: Likely Heritage In The Game

Bryson Dechambeau is a dubious figure in the realm of golf. His unconventional swing, his interest in science and information, and his forceful playing style stand out and analysis. In any case, there is no question that Dechambeau is

Bryson Dechambeau

a capable golf player who can possibly leave an enduring heritage on the game.

Dechambeau's swing is a result of his serious spotlight on biomechanics and physical science. He has concentrated on the golf swing exhaustively and has caused changes in accordance with his method that have prompted huge enhancements in his ball-striking capacity. His swing is presently one of the most impressive on the planet, and he can raise a ruckus around town long and straight with momentous consistency.

Dechambeau's interest in science and information has likewise driven him to utilize an assortment of preparation methods that are not ordinarily utilized in golf. He utilizes a send-off screen to follow his shots, and he utilizes information from his training meetings to illuminate his blueprint. This information-driven approach has assisted him with refining his swing and working on his general game.

Dechambeau's forceful playing style has likewise been a wellspring of contention. He won't hesitate to pull out all the stops, and he will make hazardous efforts that different players could avoid. This strategy has resulted in some remarkable outcomes, but it has also resulted in some notable failures.

Regardless of his debates, there is no question that Dechambeau is an amazing powerhouse in the realm of golf. He has talent, is dedicated, and is willing to push the sport to its limits. He could be a champion in the future.

Bryson Dechambeau

Here are a portion of the manners by which Dechambeau could leave an enduring inheritance on the game:

Advocating science and information in golf: Dechambeau's utilization of science and information to further develop his game could move different golf players to embrace an additional information-driven way to deal with their own preparation and planning.
Affecting golf hardware: Dechambeau's swing and his attention to power could prompt the advancement of new golf clubs and hardware that are intended to assist players with stirring things up around town further and straighter.
Having an impact on how golf is played: Dechambeau's forceful playing style could move different golf players to face more challenges and to play with more certainty.
Whether Dechambeau can accomplish his objectives, there is no question that he is a remarkable and gifted golf player who is essentially affecting the game. His inheritance will be estimated by his achievements on the course, yet it will likewise be molded by the manner in which he impacts how golf is played and how it is seen.

Bryson Dechambeau

Section 11: End

11.1: Highlights from Bryson DeChambeau's Golfing Career

Introduction: Bryson DeChambeau is an expert golf player known for his insightful and logical way of dealing with the game.

Early Years: DeChambeau was born on September 16, 1993, in Modesto, California. From a young age, he developed a love for golf.

University Achievement: He acquired noticeable qualities during his university years at Southern Methodist College (SMU), bringing home the NCAA individual title.

Single-Length Irons: DeChambeau is perceived for utilizing single-length presses, a takeoff from ordinary club arrangements.
Proficient Profession:
Professional Golf Entry: Bryson turned proficient in 2016 after a great novice vocation.

University Accomplishments: His progress in school golf included bringing home the NCAA Title and the U.S. Novice in 2015.

Bryson Dechambeau

Logical Methodology: DeChambeau's scientific mentality includes applying physical science standards to golf, acquiring him the moniker "The Researcher."

Significant Triumph: He got his most memorable significant title success at the U.S. Open in 2020, displaying his ability as a top-level golf player.
Relationships, both personal and professional:

Privacy: DeChambeau keeps his personal life, including his relationships and family, private.
Family Backing: In the same way as other competitors, he probably gets support from his family all through his profession.

Philanthropy: Competitors frequently take part in altruistic exercises, and DeChambeau might add to different causes.
Business and Supports:
Endorsements: Cobra Puma Golf, Bridgestone Golf, DraftKings, and Lexus, among others, are among DeChambeau's significant endorsement deals.
Brand Ambassadorships: His associations stretch out past item supports to address brands' qualities and development.
Wellness and Change:

Body Change: DeChambeau went through a purposeful body change in 2020, acquiring bulk to upgrade his power game.
Influence on Golf Execution: The expanded power and swing speed coming about because of his change has essentially impacted his on-course execution.

Bryson Dechambeau

Online Entertainment and Fan Cooperation:

Dynamic Presence: DeChambeau draws in fans through virtual entertainment, giving bits of knowledge into his preparation, hardware, and individual life.

Instructive Substance: He shares instructive substance connected with golf, including the science behind his strategies and gear decisions.
Community Participation:

Community involvement: While explicit subtleties might be restricted, competitors frequently participate in local area outreach, supporting youth projects, schools, and magnanimous drives.

Noble cause Occasions: Competitors, including golf players, take part in or have good cause occasions to raise assets and mindfulness for different causes.
Objectives in Golf:

Major competitions: Bringing home significant titles is a zenith objective for DeChambeau, for all intents and purposes for the majority of proficient golf players.

World No. 1 Positioning: A significant goal is to reach and keep the top spot in the Official World Golf Ranking.

Consistency and Improvement: Predictable undeniable level execution, persistent improvement, and positive off-base effect are key objectives.

Bryson Dechambeau

11.2: Bryson Dechambeau's Ongoing Effect On Golf

Bryson DeChambeau's effect on golf has been significant and expansive. He has tested customary ideas of shot-production methodology, promoted the utilization of science and innovation in golf, and touched off a discussion about the eventual fate of the game.

Reforming Distance

DeChambeau's most striking effect has been his constant quest for distance off the tee. He broadly set out on a mass structure program to expand his bulk, which empowered him to hit drives of exceptional length. His outcome in driving the ball farther than some other golf players on visit constrained courses to reexamine their plan and system, as they needed to oblige for longer methodology shots.

Sciencizing Golf

DeChambeau's way of dealing with golf has been described by his logical and scientific outlook. He has talked with biomechanics specialists, information investigators, and even NASA designers to advance his swing mechanics and hardware decisions. This information-driven approach has stretched out to his preparation routine, sustenance, and

Bryson Dechambeau

hardware choice. His readiness to analyze and embrace new advances has pushed the limits of what is conceivable in golf.

Testing Shows

DeChambeau's offbeat way of dealing with the game has affected the course as well as how golf players contemplate technique and shot production. His success has inspired younger players to adopt a more aggressive and power-focused style of play, and his willingness to give up control for distance has forced his opponents to modify their tactics.

Motivating Discussion

DeChambeau's effect on golf stretches out past the actual course. His unusual methodology has started a discussion about the eventual fate of the game, with some contending that his accentuation on distance is on a very basic level changing how golf is played and delighted in. Others assert that his pursuit of scientific innovation is propelling the game forward and increasing fan excitement.

The impact that Bryson DeChambeau has had on golf cannot be denied. He has upset the distance game, advocated the utilization of science and innovation, and tested customary ideas of the shot-production system. As his approach to the game continues to evolve and inspire new generations of golfers, his influence is likely to last for years.

Bryson Dechambeau

Made in the USA
Monee, IL
19 June 2024